The Judith Lee Stronach
Memorial Lectures
On the Teaching of Poetry

Stinson Beach, 1983

The Bancroft Library
The University of California,
Berkeley
© 2012 by the Regents of the
University of California
© Photograph of Judith, David Heiden, 1983
© Photograph of Chana Bloch, Peg Skorpinski, 1988

ISBN 978-1-893663-38-1

Learning from Translation

Chana Bloch

The Eighth Judith Lee Stronach
Memorial Lecture
On the Teaching of Poetry

May 13, 2011
The Morrison Library
The University of California,
Berkeley

The Bancroft Library
The University of California,
Berkeley

Acknowledgments

I am grateful to everyone who makes this event possible, and I especially want to thank the following people:

Zsuzsu Listro, Assistant to Tom Leonard, University Librarian, for use of the Morrison Library.

Dave Duer, Head of the Library Development Office, for permission to hold the reception in the Brown Gallery.

Beverly Ingram, also of the Development Office, who kindly assists in arranging the Morrison Room for the occasion.

Charles Faulhaber, Director, and Peter Hanff, Deputy Director of the Bancroft Library, for endorsing this series by publishing the talks.

Ron Williams, a friend, who, as Program Director for Re-entry Student and Veterans Services at Berkeley, records the talks.

Rebecca Harrach, who has catered the event each year.

Linda Snyder, who provides these beautiful flower arrangements each year.

Laura Cerruti of University of California Press, who has, since 2009, assisted the Bancroft Library in advertising and distributing the talks.

Particular thanks to Robert Hass, who gave the first lecture in 2003, and to Peter Sacks, 2004, Brenda Hillman, 2006, Sharon Olds, 2007, Carl Phillips, 2008, Philip Levine, 2009, and Peter Dale Scott, 2010. This year is noteworthy because it marks the publication of a selection of poems from Judith's unpublished manuscript, *Love is Strong As Death*, a copy of which is available to you at the end of the lecture. Thank you Brenda Hillman, Charles Legere, Chana Bloch, and Anne Barrows for selection and preparation of these poems for publication. Many thanks to Chuck Byrne for book design, to Miguel Alson for his care in printing it, and to Anne Barrows, editor.

Raymond Lifchez
May 13, 2011

Introduction

Welcome to all of you, friends, family, acquaintances old and new. This is the eighth annual Judith Lee Stronach Memorial Lecture on the Teaching of Poetry by distinguished poets. Robert Hass gave me the idea of the series soon after Judith's death, as a way to honor and to remember her, and he also gave the first lecture, "On Teaching Poetry."

As I was talking with Anne Barrows, in a conversation we have each year about the introduction to these lectures, I realized that my marriage to Judith continues, and is ongoing, that I have not finished that relationship, and that the memorial lectures provide space for the past to merge with, and to enrich, the present. It has not been possible for me to say good-bye to Judith, nor to the past we shared, nor to imagine a life without her, and so I accept that she is–however impossibly–with me today, in my connections to home, work, travel, family, friends, and to everything that gives me happiness. All marriages change over time, so mine to Judith has also changed over the years since her death in 2002, in particular with respect to my appreciation of her profoundly generous nature, her brilliance, her dedication to the betterment of the human condition, and her affirmation of both the rights and responsibilities of individuals and institutions. I have come to realize that I need to do more with my half of the relationship we shared for 37 years. These lectures are part of my commitment to Judith's memory, and to her belief that poetry can actually create change in the world.

Judith and I met in the summer of 1965, when we were students at Columbia University. Early on we discovered the passion each of us felt for our families, both large. Judith's was principally intact and living in Manhattan and Vermont. Mine had been dispersed across the country, but with a strong heartbeat in South Carolina, the original family home.

By the time I was acquainted with Judith's parents and her sister Bettina, it became essential for me to meet Elsie Lee Garthwaite, whom the family knew as "Goggy." Three days at their residence, the Play House in Manchester, and I understood how important Goggy was in the family dynamic. Indeed, hers was an essential and primary role: in the extended family, she was the centerpiece. Judith was the first girl among Goggy's eleven grandchildren–perhaps for that reason they were very close during her childhood–and it was Goggy who became the model of womanhood for Judith, and who kindled in her a deeply spiritual nature that strengthened her mind and deepened her religious practice and, in a certain nineteenth-century way, imbued in her the art and responsibility of giving–not only to philanthropic causes, but also of herself, as teacher, friend, cousin, sister, aunt, godmother, wife. Her generosity and her capacity for love were unbounded, and her relationship with Goggy was, from the beginning, remarkable. In this poem, Judith talks about a deep philosophical connection with her grandmother:

MY GOGGY, WHEN WE WALKED

I loved that she let me consider
that I might be the one to go first,
my Goggy, when we walked
to the stable and made our deal.
It was about death, about whoever
went first coming back to leave a sign
for the one left here. We walked the dirt path
and at the stable chose the place
for a message about what it is like
on the other side. Was it a rock?
About our connection, how it would survive,
how death does not separate love
from those who love. And she let me
experience the fantasy
in whoever dies first, leaving me
the possibility, so I could know then
and always that I had in me
that much love
    to cross what is not
        after all
            a divide.

Tonight we are fortunate to have Chana Kronfeld to introduce our speaker. Chana is Professor of Hebrew, Yiddish and Comparative Literature here at Berkeley. She was born and raised in Israel to refugee parents, and is the author of many books on the poetry and politics of her native Israel. Her co-translations with Chana Bloch have won significant prizes, including the PEN Translation Prize in 2001 for Yehuda Amichai's *Open, Closed, Open,* and the National Endowment for the Arts Translation Fellowship for *Hovering at a Low Altitude: The Poetry of Dahlia Ravikovitch* (Norton, 2009). Last summer she received, in Israel, the Akavyahu Lifetime Achievement Award for her research on Hebrew and Yiddish poetry. No one could introduce our speaker with more appreciation or greater authority.

Please join me in welcoming Chana Kronfeld, who will introduce Chana Bloch, this evening's speaker.

Raymond Lifchez
May 13, 2011

Learning from the Poet
An Introduction to Chana Bloch
Chana Kronfeld

I didn't know Judith Stronach personally, but have been deeply moved both by Chana's stories about her commitment to poetry and social justice, and by Ray's loving dedication to her memory. Judith's chapbook, *Love Is Strong as Death*, opens with this subtle, beautiful poem:

> TRUST IS A HAND
>
> *that does not even reach*
> *because reaching is anxiety*
> *and trust is blind*
> *vulnerability*
> *that makes a slow motion*
> *outward and, unafraid, it knows*
> *it will find another hand*
> *close by there, waiting to be touched*
> *somewhere not so dark*
> *this time on its own shoulder*
> *hand meets hand, trust gathers.*

The sense of trust in Judith's poem, where the speaker is unafraid to be vulnerable, knowing that another hand is always close by, is precisely the trust Chana and I shared as we worked on translating the intricate poetry of Yehuda Amichai and of Dahlia Ravikovitch from Hebrew into English.

Taking on a co-translation project with Chana, whose deep understanding of poetry and of translation theory seemed daunting, I was initially unprepared for how challenging the practice of this often underrated craft would turn out to be. But working together became such an intellectually thrilling and creatively satisfying experience that the apprenticeship soon developed into a collaboration that has lasted nearly fifteen years, deepening and making ever more precious a friendship that goes back two decades earlier. I will return to the art of translation at the end of my introduction, but since Chana, with her typical humility, will not talk about her own poetry, I will.

Chana's lecture will focus exclusively on her work as a translator from Hebrew and Yiddish into English. You will not hear from her that she is the author of award-winning volumes of scholarship, poetry and translation, or that her work has been celebrated, most recently, at a special session in the 2011 Modern Language Association Conference.

Her poems often make irreverent allusion to Jewish texts as well as to poems in the Western canon, offering the reader humorous yet rueful meditations on the words of others. In *Blood Honey,* her most recent collection of poems, for example, allusions to the Bible are grafted onto self-ironic references to Russian and German folk tales. One of the finest poems in the book, "Brothers," reads at first as a funny anecdote about a mother who, while playing with her boys, acts out the role of Baba Yaga, the terrifying witch of Slavic folklore, who lived in a house on chicken legs, and who–like the witch in Hansel and Gretel–had a particular fondness for children's flesh. By the middle of the last stanza, however, Baba-Yaga-as-Jewish-Mother becomes a female Abraham about to sacrifice her son, radically rewriting Genesis 22 (from which Sarah is famously absent). But it is the transition from the Binding of Isaac to the Cain and Abel story in the poem's last line that sends a shudder down my spine:

BROTHERS

When I was the Baba Yaga of the house
on my terrible chicken legs,
the children sat close on the sofa as I read,
both of them together
determined to be scared.

Careful! I cackled, stalking them
among the pillows:
You bad Russian boy,
I eat you up!
They shivered and squirmed, my delicious sons,

waiting for a mighty arm
to seize them.
I chased them screeching down the hall,
I catch you, I eat you!
my witch-blade hungry for the spurt
of laughter—

    What stopped me
even as I lifted my hand?
The stricken voice that cried: Eat him!
Eat my brother.

A concern with the Bible and its re-articulations in English poetry have linked many of Chana Bloch's scholarly and creative pursuits. She began her career at Mills College as a scholar of 17th-century English metaphysical poetry; her critical study, *Spelling the Word: George Herbert and the Bible*, won the Book of the Year Award of the Conference on Christianity and Literature, and is still considered one of the seminal studies on Herbert. In a recent interview with Zara Rabb for the *San Francisco Book Review*, Chana described how she fell in love with Herbert's poetry in graduate school in terms that playfully extend the romantic metaphor:

> We made an unlikely pair–a Jewish girl from the Bronx and a devout 17th-century Anglican minister. Herbert writes as a Christian believer who is wrestling with his faith, but in essence he is writing about the conflicts of the inner life, and I could easily relate to that; I could follow him, up to the point where he turned to Jesus for help. But that was more than enough. His poems have a beautiful dignity and candor and seriousness, along with a sharp unsparing wit.

Chana Bloch is co-translator with Ariel Bloch of the biblical Song of Songs, which was reissued as part of the Modern Library Classics Series, a translation that returns Eros, young love and vibrant dialogue to this traditionally allegorized poem. And her own poetry has been deeply engaged with the Bible, from her first book, *The Secrets of the Tribe*, which included a sequence of poems re-imagining tales from Genesis, to *Blood Honey*, whose title poem alludes to Samson "scooping sweetness from the belly of death–/ honey from the lion's carcass." In her new manuscript, *Cleopatra's Nose*, many of the poems–"The Revised Version," "Out of Eden," "Chiaroscuro," and others–continue the project of rewriting Genesis, now with an ever-expanding historical and collective perspective. Throughout her poetic work, Chana Bloch questions the biblical–and the subsequent rabbinic–obsession with separation (day from night, kosher from non-kosher, male from female, and so on). Reaching beyond these notions of binary opposition, she dares to imagine a time "before the dividing began," a holistic mindset *not* based on exclusion.

In the interview with Rabb, Chana describes the arc of her poetry, her growing concern with society's excluded others, and her heightened historical sensibility:

> In writing *Blood Honey* I felt a strong impulse to expand my field of vision. I wrote about a poet who lived fifty years in an iron lung, a Harvard student who claimed to be the Messiah, and an uncle of mine who killed a man and was proud of it.

xvii

In my new manuscript I am trying to extend my range still further. Some of the new poems are about human origins, the death of Socrates, sign language, tourism to Auschwitz. The title poem starts with an epigraph from Pascal: "If Cleopatra's nose had been shorter, the whole history of the world would have been different." I'm writing a lot about history–personal history, biblical history, European history, human history.

Chana's poetry is marked by a resistance to the elitism and obscurity all too frequently associated with the persona of the poet and with ideas about poetic language in the West. The deceptive simplicity with which "Brothers" moves from the folkloric to the biblical and the philosophical is an excellent case in point. Chana's poetry is very much in the tradition of Eastern European or Middle Eastern cultures, and perhaps of Jewish culture in particular, where poetry continues to be incorporated into the fabric of everyday life. In the interview, she articulates this explicitly as a poetics of clarity, at least as far as the first rhetorical impression of the poem is concerned. Note that she is not arguing for a poetry of surface, but is rather claiming that a poem can–and should!–be clear and multi-layered at one and the same time: "I value clarity–an old-fashioned virtue–and concision. I like poetry that appears to be clear on the surface, but with unexpected depths."

Chana Bloch has had a distinguished career as a poet and translator. Her four poetry collections are *The Secrets of the Tribe,* which was a finalist for the Yale Younger Poets Award; *The Past Keeps Changing; Mrs. Dumpty,* which won the Felix Pollak Prize in Poetry; and *Blood Honey,* which received the Poetry Society of America's Alice Fay di Castagnola Award. *The Selected Poetry of Yehuda Amichai,* which she translated with Stephen Mitchell, is by all accounts the authoritative selection of Amichai's poetry available so far in English. I was fortunate to collaborate with her in translating Amichai's last book, *Open Closed Open,* which won the PEN Translation Prize, and most recently *Hovering at a Low Altitude: The Collected Poetry of Dahlia Ravikovitch.*

Chana has a B.A. from Cornell, an M.A. in Judaic Studies and one in English Literature from Brandeis, and a Ph.D. in English from Berkeley. Professor Emerita of English at Mills College, where she directed the Creative Writing Program, she is now the Poetry Editor of *Persimmon Tree.* Many of her poems and translations have been set to music, including *Chana's Story,* music composed by David Del Tredici, which premiered at the Yerba Buena Center for the Arts in San Francisco, and Jorge Liderman's cantata, *The Song of Songs,* performed by the San Francisco Contemporary Music Players and the U.C. Berkeley Chamber Chorus. You may not know that she has recently also become a movie star, and can be seen discussing our translation of Dahlia Ravikovitch in *Traduire*, a documentary by the noted Israeli-French filmmaker Nurith Aviv that premiered in Paris last year. Despite the Parisian connection, this native New Yorker loves living in Berkeley. Chana has two grown sons, Benjamin and Jonathan, and is married to Dave Sutter, with whom she shares a love of poetry, art, and music. She has, in addition, a near-total recall of all of Shakespeare's plays.

Finally, let me say a few words about what it has been like to collaborate with Chana on our translations of Yehuda Amichai's *Open Closed Open* and the *Collected Poetry of Dahlia Ravikovitch*, each of which took several years of intensive, exhilarating labor to complete. I have come to treasure our shared commitment to true collaboration, and an abhorrence of competitiveness, and to relish our debates over every turn of phrase: you never get as close to the texture of a poem as when you are translating it with Chana Bloch. With her unparalleled open-mindedness, she welcomes every discussion, every disagreement, from the most minute detail of rhythm and word play to the largest issues of cross-cultural negotiation. She has said that when we work together she often feels as if forces much larger than us–American and Israeli culture and history as a whole–are encountering each other at our desk. Indeed, the moments when these encounters become most palpable are also the most thrilling–intellectually and creatively–for both of us.

But when it came to turning my pedantic, academic literal translations into poetry, Chana was nothing short of a miracle worker. Often I would say at the end of a long day of working side by side, "You know, Chana, I don't think this is actually translatable." Sure enough, the following morning there would be Chana, a smile on her face, with a draft marked in different colors to highlight the play of sound, or an allusion that heightened the literary resonance of the poem in English. Let me close with one brief example. In Dahlia Ravikovitch's poem, "On Account of a King," a parable set in the times of the Roman conquests, the soldiers are described in the Hebrew as having no time "to pamper their bodies under eiderdown." That sounded really clunky in English, whereas the Hebrew was uniquely fresh and beautiful in its use of archaisms; I was ready to give up. But the next day Chana came back with "to dally where the beds are soft," echoing *Antony and Cleopatra*–and all of a sudden, we had a poem!

Thank you, dearest friend, for the gift of our collaboration and the treasure that is your poetry.

Chana Bloch

Learning from Translation

Chana Bloch

Thank you, Ray, for inviting me to speak here tonight, and thank you, Chana, for your very generous introduction. I don't think you and I have ever resolved the issue of who is learning from whom, but I'm grateful for everything I've learned from you about Yiddish and Hebrew and translation and poetry (you are my most demanding critic!). What I am going to say this evening depends to a great extent on our deeply gratifying work together since 1997. You will recognize some of your words, which are bound up inextricably with my own, always to my benefit and my delight.

    I knew Judith Stronach through a poetry reading group–one of Berkeley's flourishing cottage industries. Our group meets once a month to read and discuss a book of poetry, often poetry in translation, from Homer to Hikmet. I remember the evening we read the work of Czeslaw Milosz at Judith's home, and I still have, tucked between the pages of his *Collected Poetry,* the list of poems that Judith suggested. Two weeks before she died, we read Tomas Tranströmer's work at my house. Judith sent a warm note the next day, thanking me for bringing his poetry to the group and saying how much she had enjoyed the discussion. Poetry seemed very much alive for her then; as Ray has said, it was a kind of lifeline for her. Two weeks later we came together in mourning, and read *her* poems.

Tonight you have in your hands a selection of Judith's poems. She chose as its title a verse from the Song of Songs: "Love Is Strong as Death," *azza ka-mavet ahava* (Songs, 8:6), a bold simile spoken by the Shulamite, who makes that claim for love's power. Judith alludes to it in the poem about her grandmother that Ray just read: "death does not separate love / from those who love." In offering the Stronach Memorial Lectures to the community, Ray is reasserting that claim, confirming that the connection does indeed survive. This lecture series in Judith's name pays loving tribute to her spirit, and I am honored to be part of it. Here is Judith's poem:

MY GOGGY, WHEN WE WALKED

I loved that she let me consider
that I might be the one to go first,
my Goggy, when we walked
to the stable and made our deal.
It was about death, about whoever
went first coming back to leave a sign
for the one left here. We walked the dirt path
and at the stable chose the place
for a message about what it is like
on the other side. Was it a rock?
About our connection, how it would survive,
how death does not separate love
from those who love. And she let me
experience the fantasy
in whoever dies first, leaving me
the possibility, so I could know then
and always that I had in me
that much love
      to cross what is not
           after all
                a divide.

I am struck by the child's curiosity about "what it is like / on the other side," and her discovery that love would enable her, through the power of empathy and imagination, "to cross what is not / after all / a divide."

My subject this evening is translation, so I will be talking about border crossings of a different kind. To translate, as literary theorists remind us, is literally to "carry across," from the Latin *trans* + *ferre*–that is, to carry something across the barriers of language and culture that separate us from an unknown country on the other side. Those barriers are generally invisible to the reader, though they are all too clear to the translator who must work her way across or around them. The reader who wishes to experience a translation in all its particularity needs to have some notion of what those barriers are.

We've all heard the nasty quips. "Poetry is what gets lost in translation," said Robert Frost; "translators are traitors," say the Italians; in French, where the word *traduction* is feminine, the expression, *"les belles infidèles"* implies that a translation can be either beautiful or faithful–*belle* or *fidele*–but not both. All too often, publishers, editors, and reviewers treat translators with disrespect. A translation is seen as the handmaiden of the (male) original, a creature of a lesser order, fashioned from the primal rib. You may be wondering why any sensible person would choose to engage in this much-maligned art. I must confess: I've been at it for fifty years, and it has been one of the joys of my life.

First of all, there is the pleasure of reading. Translating a poem is a particularly intimate form of reading, close and slow. Once you and that poem start living together, you get to know its pulse and body heat, a sensual pleasure. Then there's the intellectual charge that comes from problem-solving: the most resistant passages often yield the greatest satisfaction. That kind of work keeps the blood circulating in the brain. As a remedy for aging, it's even better than drinking red wine. And there's food for the spirit, too, when you live in the presence of something larger than yourself. George Steiner has written, "Without [translation], we would live in arrogant parishes bordered by silence." Berkeley is home to almost as many translators as poets, and I think they would say amen.

I was drawn to translation because I am a poet. As a young writer, in a workshop with Robert Lowell, I submitted, along with my own poems, some translations of Abraham Sutzkever, the great Yiddish poet who died last year. (We commemorated his ninetieth birthday here in the Morrison Library in 2003.) Lowell told me, "You can learn to write from your own translations." His suggestion provided more than the title of this talk: it proved to be *the* most helpful advice I ever received about writing. Later I discovered that W. S. Merwin had heard the same thing from Pound. If he wanted to be a writer he should write every day, Pound said, but since he was too young to have anything worth writing about, he ought to translate. Pound spoke of the value of translation "as a means of continually sharpening a writer's awareness of the possibilities of his own language."

A translator needs to know at least one language very well: her own. You might say that translation is a form of apprenticeship–not to a master craftsman, but to the genius of the language itself. When you translate you are constantly choosing among alternatives in order to convey meaning, register, image, mood, music; each time you choose, you are exercising muscles that you need in shaping your own work. It's a strenuous but efficient way of teaching yourself to write. For that reason, when I taught poetry workshops or courses about poetry, I always made a point of including translations. In class we compared different versions of poems by Wang Wei, Akhmatova, Baudelaire, Rilke, Lorca, and Celan as a way of learning how a poem is put together, what makes it tick, how much of it can be gotten into English.

Though I had studied other languages, I had a specific reason for choosing to translate from Yiddish and Hebrew. I grew up as a first-generation American, living between two cultures. My parents came to this country from tiny villages, *shtetlekh,* in the Ukraine. At home they spoke English, not Yiddish, but they sent me to a Yiddish *folkshul* every day after school. (Not to Hebrew school, like my brother: Hebrew belonged to the men and the boys.) I began to study Hebrew as an undergraduate at Cornell and as a graduate student of Judaic Studies at Brandeis, and continued during two extended stays in Jerusalem. In my twenties, I discovered that translation offered me a way of honoring the creativity in these two languages, more meaningful by far than the "nostalgia *yiddishkayt*" that often passes for Jewish identity. Once I was engaged in this work, I felt a responsibility to help save what might otherwise be lost, and to contribute something of substance to American-Jewish culture.

I've chosen to talk about translating from Yiddish poetry and prose, and Hebrew poetry, Biblical and contemporary. Each of these subjects presents a different set of challenges, any one of which would suffice for an hour's lecture, or a semester's course. I wanted to touch on them together, not only because they figure in my personal history, but also, more important, because they are intertwined–at times fiercely (some of you will know about the "language wars")–in Jewish literary history. Chana Kronfeld's pioneering research and teaching about this "bilingual literature" has transformed the study of Hebrew and Yiddish in the United States, Britain and Israel.

Yiddish began its life about a thousand years ago in Northern Italy, and then evolved in the Rhineland as a Germanic language with Romance and Hebrew-Aramaic components, written in Hebrew characters. As the Jews migrated eastward, between the thirteenth century and the sixteenth, Yiddish absorbed elements of Slavic as well. In Eastern Europe, Hebrew-Aramaic was *loshn koydesh*, "the holy tongue," reserved for the man's world of study and worship; Yiddish was *mame-loshn*, "the mother tongue" of home and marketplace, of everyday life. Yiddish was originally called *Yiddish-taytsh*, or simply *Taytsh*, from the word for "German," *Deutsch*. *Fartaytshn* meant to gloss a Hebrew text by giving a word-by-word equivalent in the Jewish vernacular–at first Aramaic, later Yiddish, Ladino, and other languages. In modern Yiddish, *fartaytshn* is still one of the verbs for "translate," revealing the Jewish nexus between translation and interpretation.

Isaac Bashevis Singer recognized the uniqueness of Yiddish in his Nobel Prize speech in 1978:

> The high honor bestowed upon me by the Swedish Academy is also a recognition of the Yiddish language–a language of exile, without a land, without frontiers, not supported by any government, a language which possesses no words for weapons, ammunition, military exercises, war tactics; a language that was despised by both Gentiles and emancipated Jews…. There are some who call Yiddish a dead language, but so was Hebrew called for two thousand years…. Yiddish has not yet said its last word.

A stirring prophecy, worthy of a master of fantasy. In sober fact, Hitler and Stalin murdered the writers and readers and speakers of Yiddish, dealing a catastrophic blow as well to the language itself. In America, Yiddish survives mostly in a debased form, in jokes and wisecracks and the handful of words that have made it into Webster's: *schlep, schmooze, schmear, schmatte, shtick, schlock*. This familiarity among the general population is proclaimed in some quarters as a cultural achievement. Today, Yiddish is spoken in the ultra-Orthodox community, and, one might say, is enjoying an afterlife in the academy, taught in many colleges here and abroad, but all of that is not the same as being a living language. Modern Yiddish literature flourished only from the end of the nineteenth century until the middle of the twentieth. As Benjamin Harshav put it: "a brilliant performance and… a tragic exit from an empty hall."

The Yiddish writers I translated shared an urgency to be heard that was different from anything I'd encountered among writers of English. For the former, translation was a necessary condition of survival. Who, after all, was reading them in Yiddish? Or who would be, in the future? Two of the major figures of post-war Yiddish literature in the U.S. were Isaac Bashevis

Singer (1904-1991), who had an international reputation, and Jacob Glatstein (1896-1971), hardly known outside the Yiddish world. Cynthia Ozick has written a painful and hilarious novella, *Envy; or, Yiddish in America,* about Ostrover, the fiction writer (a thinly-veiled portrait of Singer), and Edelshtein, the poet (a harsh caricature of Glatstein), the former reaching a large audience through his translators, the latter desperate because he has none. As Ozick frames the issue:

> Ostrover's glory was exactly in this: that he required translators! Though he wrote only in Yiddish, his fame was American, national, international. They considered him a "modern." Ostrover was free of the prison of Yiddish! The unhappy Edelshtein beweeps his outcast state: And why Ostrover? Why not somebody else?…Ostrover should be the only one? Everyone else sentenced to darkness, Ostrover alone saved?

I read Ozick's novella with some interest because I had translated both Singer and Glatstein, and because the young girl whom the Yiddish poet begs to translate his work ("twenty-three years old…an American girl… crazy for literature") is called Hannah. But the pathetic Yiddish poet in Ozick's story bears no resemblance to the real-life Glatstein, nor am I Ozick's Hannah. Jacob Glatstein was a poet of great distinction whose work I admired.

It was not by chance that the first poem I translated was Glatstein's "Smoke" (*"Roykh"*). Published just after the war, in 1946, it is an indictment of the God that failed:

> Durkhn krematorie koymen
> Kroyzt aroyf a yid tsum asik yoymin.
> Un vi nor der roykh farshvindt,
> Knoyln aroyf zayn vayb un kind.
>
> Un oybn, in di himlishe hoykhn,
> Veynen, benken heylike roykhn.
> Got, dort vu du bist do,
> Dortn zaynen mir ale oykh nishto.

> *From the crematory flue*
> *A Jew aspires to the Holy One.*
> *And when the smoke of him is gone,*
> *His wife and children filter through.*

Above us, in the height of sky,
Saintly billows weep and wait.
God, wherever you may be,
There all of us are also not.

The bitter irony in that voice gripped me, haunted me, would not let go until I had turned it into English.

Glatstein's form was a given: the clipped rhythms and tightly-rhymed quatrains are a way of containing grief and despair. What stopped me were the neologisms in stanza 1, nouns (*kroyz, knoly*) that Glatstein turns into verbs (*kroyzt, knolyn*) to suggest the motion of the smoke winding upwards like a *kroyz*, a "curl" (of smoke or hair), unwinding like a *knoyl*, a "ball" (of thread or string). Literal equivalents seemed to me clumsy and pedantic, and they lacked the bite of the Yiddish. I chose "aspires" and "filter through" for their ironic edge; "aspires" to evoke the ideal of the aspiring mind, and "filter through" to suggest the harrowing domesticity of Glatstein's metaphor. But I had never done this thing called translation before, and I wasn't at all sure I was doing it right.

In the Introduction to his *Imitations* (1958)–not really translations but rather adaptations of European poetry–Robert Lowell writes that "the usual reliable translator gets the literal meaning but misses the tone, and…in poetry, tone is, of course, everything. I have been reckless with literal meaning," he goes on to say, "and labored hard to get the tone." I was worried: had I let go of the literal meaning in order to get the tone? I sent my version to Glatstein with a letter half-apologizing for the freedoms I had taken. He wrote back at once with great enthusiasm, inviting me to translate more of his work. And so I learned at the start two of the cardinal rules of translation: first, it's not just a matter of finding word-for-word equivalents, and second, it's the tone that makes the music. Translation, as the Jewish textual tradition teaches us, is a form of interpretation, and to a greater or lesser degree, it necessarily involves transformation.

Despite his considerable achievements, Isaac Bashevis Singer was viewed with disdain in Yiddishist literary circles, and not simply because of writers' envy, as Ozick's story suggests. Naomi Seidman discusses the response to Singer in her wide-ranging and illuminating book about translation, *Faithful Renderings: Jewish-Christian Difference and the Politics of Translation*. In the words of Irving Saposnik, a critic she quotes, Singer was "an entrepreneur, a skillful marketer of both his image and his imagination," who gave the American audience just what it wanted: "sharp edges were smoothed, ethnic quirks turned into old-world charm...and Bashevis crossed over from the mundane obscurity of a Yiddish writer to being the darling of the literary world." Seidman has an apt phrase for this kind of crossover: she calls it "translation-as-assimilation."

Saul Bellow brought Singer to national attention with his pungent, idiomatic translation of "Gimpel the Fool," published in 1953 in the *Partisan Review*. Bellow conveys the feel of Singer's Yiddish, but, as Naomi Seidman and Janet Hadda have noted, he quietly omits what might be offensive to a Gentile reader: the derogatory anti-Christian epithets *shiksa* and *goy*, along with a line that implies the virgin birth is foolishness no Jew would ever believe. Bellow's partner-in-crime, Eliezer Greenberg, gets the blame for those omissions, but I can't help wondering if Singer himself had anything to do with it.

Seidman's chapter on Singer got me thinking about my own experience. Thanks to the detective efforts of Paul Hamburg, the Judaica librarian at U. C. Berkeley, who tracked my versions of Singer to the U.T. Austin library, I now have copies of a few drafts of the stories I translated. Even in that limited sample I found some evidence for what the critics were saying. Singer worked closely with me, as he did with all his translators. We would meet over prune Danish at the Automat on the Upper West Side to go over my drafts. Having checked those against the originals, I can now see that where I missed nuances of the Yiddish, he did not bother to correct me. His changes were mostly directed at making the stories more accessible to an American audience. I had deliberately retained a few Yiddish words, assuming that the reader would be able to infer their meaning from the context. Singer changed *rebbetsin* ("rabbi's wife") to "saint," and *Mogen Dovid* to "Star of David." He crossed out *le-chayim* and wrote "to your health," but then thought better of it. Where one of his characters says, "She married a Litvak," he crossed out "Litvak" and wrote "Lithuanian." But a *Litvak* is not just a person from Lithuania, or Latvia or Russia; it's a Jewish character type scorned by the *Galitzyaner* Jews as a cold rationalist, lacking in emotional depth. (Czeslaw Milosz was a Lithuanian, but he was *not* a Litvak!)

My translations of Singer are billed as a collaboration between me and Elizabeth Pollet, but that wasn't exactly the case. In fact, Singer subsequently submitted my versions to Pollett, an American-Jewish novelist, for further editing; her task was apparently to make the stories read like current American fiction, so she upgraded the sentence structure in places where I had left a trace of Yiddish syntax. Singer's readiness to have his originals retouched reveals how eager he was to reach an American audience. When we worked together, I was too much a beginner to question his approach. Today it's clear to me that what gets lost in translation-by-assimilation is the distinctive savor of the culture, just as it does in the bland versions of ethnic foods prepared for the American palate.

Lost in Translation is the title of a memoir by Eva Hoffman; the subtitle is *A Life in a New Language* (1989). Hoffman writes about emigrating with her family in 1959, when she was a girl of thirteen, from Cracow to Vancouver, where she was to acquire, along with a new language, "a whole new geography of emotions." Her memoir demonstrates again and again the inseparability of language from culture. In one of her most telling anecdotes, Hoffman ponders her relationship with her American boyfriend: "Should you marry him? the question comes in English. Yes. Should you marry him? the question echoes in Polish. No." Asking the question in a different language prompts an entirely different set of cultural assumptions and elicits an antithetical response. Recent research on psycholinguistics confirms as much: when bilingual people switch from one language to another, they start thinking differently, too. A Polish-speaking Jew, Hoffman had to reinvent herself in English: as she put it, "I have to translate myself without becoming assimilated"–a good plan of action for anyone engaged in translation.

It is more difficult to translate poetry than prose, and considerably more difficult to translate an ancient text than a contemporary one, which is to say that translating the Song of Songs proved to be an unusually rewarding project. If you have a question when you are translating a living author, you can often get the answer straight from (pardon me) the source's mouth. When you are translating an ancient text, there's no author to consult, and there are many more questions than answers. Who wrote the Song? Certainly not King Solomon. Could it have been a woman? When was it written? Was it a collection of lyrics or a unified whole? I was fortunate to have as my collaborator Ariel Bloch, who was a professor of Semitic linguistics at U. C. Berkeley. We dealt with those questions, and others as perplexing, in our Introduction, presenting the evidence for our conclusions while admitting that finally there is no certainty.

The Song of Songs celebrates the sexual awakening of a young, unmarried woman and her lover; it is the only love poem that has survived from ancient Israel. While it was most likely composed as a poem about erotic love, the rabbis read it as an allegory about the love of God and the people of Israel; this interpretation, along with the attribution to King Solomon, helped it to survive the final cut of the canon-makers. The Church Fathers in turn read the Song as a dialogue between Christ and his Bride, the Church. Once it became part of the Holy Scriptures, the Song demanded exegesis befitting its holiness, and religious interpretations of one kind or another prevailed for two millennia. Some of the more extravagant "findings" of the exegetes now seem very curious: the Shulamite's two breasts, for example, were said to signify Moses and Aaron, or the Old and the New Testaments. The passion in the Song rises at times to 120 degrees in the shade, but in the long history of exegesis and translation, the temperature drops precipitously.

Exegetes and translators commonly presented the young lovers as yearning for one another from a respectable distance, though in doing so they were ignoring the plain sense of the Hebrew. In 4:16, the Shulamite invites her beloved: "Let my lover come into his garden / and taste its delicious fruit," and he replies:

> *I have come into my garden,*
> *my sister, my bride,*
> *I have gathered my myrrh and my spices,*
> *I have eaten from the honeycomb,*
> *I have drunk the milk and the wine. (Song 5:1)*

The verb "to come into" or "to enter" often has a sexual meaning in Biblical Hebrew. And the metaphors of feasting suggest fulfillment, especially since the verbs are in the perfect tense (*bati, ariti, akhalti, shatiti:* "I have come, I have gathered, I have eaten, I have drunk"), which signifies a completed action, i.e., consummation. Translators who resort to a noncommittal present tense (I come, I gather, I eat, I drink) or an infinitive construction (I have come to gather) are toning down the lover's exultant song of gratified desire. And the Shulamite, a young woman as spirited and assertive as Juliet, gets subdued as well. In almost every translation up to our own day (the King James Version is a notable exception), we find her wearing a veil, a reading not supported by the Hebrew. That incongruous veil, like the fig leaf of Renaissance painting and sculpture, is a sign of the discomfort of the exegetes. Even contemporary translations may blunt the full intensity of the text because, as so often in the history of translation, misreadings get passed down uncritically from one generation to the next.

The best known English translation is, of course, the King James Version (KJV, 1611), celebrating its four-hundredth anniversary this year. The KJV is a monumental achievement, with an immense impact on our literature, and its rendering of the Song has been justly beloved by generations of readers for its rich textures and resounding cadences–not the usual product of committee work. However, advances in Biblical scholarship during the past four centuries have shown many of its readings to be in error, including some of the best-known verses, such as "Stay me with flagons, comfort me with apples" (Song 2:5) or "terrible as an army with banners" (Song 6:10). And its language is often dated, for example, "I am sick of love" (Song 2:5) or the unfortunate "My beloved put in his hand by the hole of the door, and my bowels were moved for him" (Song 5:4). The language of the KJV was conceived for liturgical purposes and was somewhat archaic even in the seventeenth century; its formal, stately music doesn't convey the heat, the speed, the erotic intensity of the original. One would hardly know that this is a poem about young lovers.

Deciphering the Hebrew text proved to be more difficult than Ariel and I had anticipated. The Song is one of the most enigmatic books in the Bible, far more obscure and problematic than a reader of English might suppose, in part because it has an unusually high proportion of rare words and constructions. Resolving the puzzles in the Hebrew was Ariel's assignment. Once the two of us had a reasonably clear sense of what the Hebrew was saying, it was my task to embody that reading–unexpurgated–in English that sounded like poetry.

A poem about erotic love no longer seems shocking, and the Shulamite, with her veil off, is a figure we recognize. In our day it is the innocence of the Song that has the power to surprise–a freshness of spirit now all but lost to us. The language of the Song is at once voluptuous and reticent, an effect achieved through the medium of metaphor. The Shulamite's invitation–"Let my lover come into his garden / and taste its delicious fruit" (4:16)–is characteristic both in what it asserts and what it leaves unexpressed. Ariel and I felt that none of the English translations conveyed the rare combination of sensuousness and delicacy that makes the Hebrew so captivating.

Seamus Heaney writes in the Introduction to his translation of *Beowulf*: "It is one thing to find lexical meanings for the words…but it is quite another thing to find the tuning fork that will give you the note and pitch for the overall music of the work." Searching for the proper register in English took us through a cartonful of drafts. A change in any one verse often demanded a change in several others. But then translation is labor-intensive work. It requires not just imagination, but also patience and perseverance (some would call it obsessiveness). By trial and error we found our way to the stylistic register we sought, steering a course between what Robert Alter calls "the extremes of clunky sexual explicitness and the pastels of greeting-card poetry, which are equal if opposite violations of the original."

Language that is too explicit cheapens the Song. Here is how a distinguished scholar cranked up the heat in his translation in the Anchor Bible Series: "Your vulva [is] a rounded crater; / May it never lack punch!" (Song 7:3) This translation, with its three howlers, illustrates why a translator needs to be sensitive to questions of style. By "crater" this scholar meant a mixing bowl, and by "punch" he meant spiced wine, though it seems he did not stop to think about the associations of those words in English. But "vulva" takes the prize. The sexual organs are never named in the Song, though they are of course suggested many times over. The word *shorerekh* means "your navel," not "your vulva"; in any case, the anatomical term "vulva" is barbaric, given the elegantly evocative language of the Song. Our translation reads:

> *Your navel is the moon's*
> *bright drinking cup.*
> *May it brim with wine!*

"The pastels of greeting-card poetry" might well describe a recent verse translation that attempts to universalize the Song: the Shulamite becomes a "princess"; the daughters of Jerusalem, "city women"; Ein Gedi, an "oasis"; the rose of Sharon, "a wildflower thriving" in "sandy earth"; Mount Gilead, "the slopes"; Mount Carmel a "majestic mountain"; and "the tower of Lebanon / that looks toward Damascus" a "tower that overlooks the hills." All the distinctive markers have been deleted–the place names that situate the action, along with their music, as sonorous in English as it is in Hebrew. What is the point of domesticating the ancient and the foreign? It's like tourist travel made easy: the travel agent smoothes the way so you are as comfortable as if you had never left home.

The concision of Biblical Hebrew, most pronounced in the poetic books, and a special delight in the Song, is often the first casualty in translation. Biblical Hebrew is an inflected language, which means that it does much of its semantic work with prefixes and suffixes, the conjugation of verbs and declension of nouns. The compact phrase *bati le-gani* requires six words in English: "I-have-come into-my-garden." (Song 5:1) The last thing one should do is pad lines to fill out some rhyme scheme or metrical scheme, foreign to Biblical Hebrew, which would constrict or contort their natural rhythmical flow. The text itself offers some clues to the translator. The Shulamite invites her lover, "Take me by the hand, let us run together" (Song 1:4: *moshkheni acharekha narutza*), and she describes him as "a gazelle, a wild stag...bounding over the mountains" (Song 2:9, 8). The young lovers of the Song are full of the animal energy of youth, and the Hebrew lines are accordingly sinewy, graceful, lithe. How to convey that energy in English? "Think like a deer," a friend advised.

The opening verses of the Song set the tone, so each word counts:

> *Kiss me, make me drunk with your kisses!*
> *Your dodim*
> *are better than wine. (Song 1:2)*

The plural noun *dodim* is almost always translated as "love," which is imprecise and evasive, given that it refers specifically to lovemaking. *Dodim* occurs only three other times in the Bible: in the Book of Proverbs, where a seductive woman tempts a clueless young man, "Come, let us drink our fill of *dodim*, let us make love all night long, for my husband is not at home" (Prov. 7:18-19); as well as in Ezekiel's denunciations of Jerusalem as an unfaithful wife or a harlot (Ezek. 16:8 and 23:17). Since *dodim* in the Song clearly refers to an *activity*, not just a state of mind, we translated it with the verbal noun "loving": "Your sweet loving / is better than wine."

I'd like to look briefly at a lyric spoken by each of the lovers. Here, in our translation, is the Shulamite in her passionate and dramatic mode:

> *Now he has brought me*
> *to the house of wine,*
> *and his flag over me is love.*
>
> *Let me lie among vine blossoms,*
> *in a bed of apricots!*
> *I am in the fever of love.*
>
> *His left hand beneath my head,*
> *his right arm*
> *holding me close.*

*Daughters of Jerusalem, swear to me
by the gazelles, by the deer in the field,
that you will never awaken love
until it is ripe. (Song 2:4-7)*

Nearly every word in 2:5 gave us pause. "Stay me with flagons, comfort me with apples" is the well-known King James translation of *samkhuni ba-ashishot, rapduni ba-tapuchim*. However, *samkhuni* and *rapduni* are not verbs of feeding, as is commonly assumed, but rather of upholstery, as the roots *smk* and *rpd* reveal. The implied image here is of plumping up a bed in preparation for an erotic encounter, as in Proverbs 7:16-17: "I have spread my couch with fine Egyptian linen; I have perfumed my bed with myrrh, aloes and cinnamon." (The seductive woman in Proverbs sounds a bit like the Shulamite, though of course *her* come-hither is presented as a cautionary tale.)

Some readers have objected, "Put the apples back in the Song of Songs," demanding "an apple for an apple"–reparations for the loss of Paradise– though in the Garden of Eden, of course, there is no "apple," simply the generic "fruit." *Tappuach* means "apple" in modern Hebrew, and it has usually been translated as "apple" in the Song, but botanists believe that it more likely refers to the apricot, a fruit that has been abundant in Israel since Biblical times. The apple tree is not native to the area, and was introduced comparatively recently. Wild apples are small, hard and acidic, while apricots are soft, golden, fleshy and fragrant. Since the fruit of the apricot tree is an image for the lover himself (Song 2:3), "apricot" is more suitable on all counts.

"I am sick of love," is the King James translation of *cholat ahava ani*. In the King's English of the seventeenth century, that would have meant "stricken by passion"; in colloquial English today, "I am sick of love" means "leave me alone, I've had enough." Many translations try to salvage this phrase by putting a patch on it, but "I am sick with love" sounds to me like bad English; another possibility, "I am faint with love," is much too Victorian. I can still remember the day when, after months of wrestling with this verse, the word "fever" occurred to me: "I am in the fever of love." I was so high that I went out the door and ran four miles.

And now the young lover, who speaks these lines in praise of the Shulamite:

You have ravished my heart,
my sister, my bride,
ravished me with one glance of your eyes,
one link of your necklace.

And oh, your sweet loving,
my sister, my bride.
The wine of your kisses, the spice
of your fragrant oils.

Your lips are honey, honey and milk
are under your tongue,
your clothes hold the scent of Lebanon. (Song 4:9-11)

Specificity is always preferred where the Hebrew is specific, as in *dodim* ("loving"), but it may be misleading where the Hebrew is indeterminate. Where the lover speaks of the Shulamite's *salmah* (Song 4:11), we couldn't be sure precisely what she was wearing, but the real question was how to convey whatever it was in English. "Cloak" and "mantle" seemed too old-fashioned, "gown" and "garment" too formal, "robes" too regal, "tunic" too Greek, "dress" too contemporary. Such terms are time-bound, culture-bound; they convey nuances that are alien to the Hebrew, and are constricting, in the way that illustrations in a book often limit rather than stir the imagination. A prominent New York artist was commissioned by Random House to prepare illustrations which, thankfully, were not used in our book: he had the Shulamite wearing a red sundress with spaghetti straps.

In a poetic (as opposed to a scholarly) translation, sound and rhythm are essential elements, part of the sensual experience of the reader. The Hebrew of the Song is rich in assonance and alliteration. Sometimes we were able to suggest the play of sound in the Hebrew:

Nofet tittofnah siftotayikh kallah
devash ve-chalav tachat leshonekh
ve-reach salmotayikh ke-reach levanon.

Your lips are honey, honey and milk
are under your tongue,
your clothes hold the scent of Lebanon. (Song 4:11)

But it wasn't always possible to replicate the music of a given verse, so we used alliteration and assonance wherever we could; for example:

> *They beat me, they bruised me,*
> *they tore the shawl from my shoulders,*
> *those watchmen of the walls. (Song 5:8)*

Translating an ancient text is in some ways analogous to the process of restoring a work of art that has been dulled by time. In the 1980s a team of conservators examined the frescoes on the ceiling of the Sistine Chapel, using infrared light to penetrate the surface, and then, with meticulous care, set about removing five centuries of grime, soot, smoke, and varnish. Their work revealed unexpectedly brilliant colors, hues of turquoise and orange that seemed quite unlike Michelangelo–that is, unlike the Michelangelo of tradition, who was thought to favor a much more subdued palette. The colors of the Song in our translation are brighter, its music more sensuous, than in other versions. Those charms of the Song are not our invention; they belong to the pleasures of the original Hebrew. Our aim was to restore in English the passion and intensity, the magical freshness, of this great ancient poem.

In modern Hebrew poetry, the Song of Songs became the model for a boldly secular eroticism, explicitly challenging the allegorical interpretations, notably in the work of Yehuda Amichai (1924-2000), one of the great poets–indeed, one of the great love poets–of our time. His poetry is enormously popular in Israel–recited at weddings and funerals, taught in the schools, set to music–and it has been translated into over forty languages, including Catalan, Estonian, Korean, Serbo-Croatian, and Vietnamese. When I first met Amichai in Berkeley in the late 1960s, I had already found my way to his poems, attracted by their emotional vitality, their salty wit and skeptical intelligence.

Translating from modern Hebrew presents an unusual challenge. Hebrew was revived as a vernacular only about a hundred years ago, and modern Hebrew preserves, even in everyday speech, the resonance of all its historical layers. Even the simplest words remain charged with ancient, often sacred meanings. A common term like *davar*, which means "word" or "thing," can also refer to a prophetic vision; *makom*, "place," and *shem*, "name," are familiar ways of referring to God. The theological connotations of Biblical and rabbinic language are present everywhere in Amichai's poetry, often as the object of his irony. Hebrew verbs and nouns are typically based on tri-consonantal roots that embody some general idea. Since the root system of Hebrew creates a kind of "component awareness," the archaic layers of the language, as well as new-minted expressions, are generally transparent to readers. Amichai is able to draw upon the whole history of the language–Biblical, rabbinic, medieval, and modern–alluding irreverently to texts from earlier periods without any sense of strain, and relying on his audience to recognize the allusions.

Biblical expressions that sound perfectly natural in colloquial Hebrew may seem stilted or bookish in an English poem. One can suggest some of the semantic effects possible in Hebrew, for example, by juxtaposing words of Germanic or Latinate origin, though it would be jarring to introduce a word from *Beowulf* or *The Canterbury Tales* into a poem in colloquial English. What's more, Amichai's dialogue with the Bible, the Midrash and the liturgy is only part of the story. He draws equally on vernacular Israeli culture–popular songs, Jewish jokes, nursery rhymes, doggerel, children's games, legal language, military slang. He was influenced by English poetry as well; in fact, it was his chance discovery of the *Faber Book of Modern Verse* that first got him started as a writer. Amichai's poetry is noted for its playfulness and wit, and it moves easily from one stylistic register to another. The norms of English tend to resist rapid shifts in register, so a translation that attempts to reproduce every nuance of his Hebrew would very likely seem muddled.

Amichai himself would acknowledge this readily. What's more, his view of the relation between poet and translator calls into question the usual hierarchy. He doesn't regard the poet as inspired creator, acclaimed for his originality, as in the Romantic tradition, but quite the contrary: as a *translator* of sorts, a simple link in the chain of transmission. The poet-as-translator appears in an early poem, "And Let Us Not Get Excited" (1962), as a middleman who passes on "words from one person to another, one tongue to other lips / ... the way a father passes on / the facial features of his dead father to his son." And in a late poem, "Conferences, Conferences: Malignant Words, Benign Speech" (1998), the poet-as-translator figures prominently, confronting the institutional abuse of language in politics or academia, and toiling to "make honey, like bees, from all the buzz and babble." Notice how Amichai's linking of poetry and translation dismisses the common clichés about translation as betrayal and loss.

In closing, I'd like to return to those two issues, which bedevil discussions about translation: what does "free" mean? And what exactly gets "lost"? My illustrations will come from two of Amichai's love poems.

"A Precise Woman" appears in *The Selected Poetry* (1986), which I translated with Stephen Mitchell. At that time I was living in Jerusalem. Stephen worked with Chana Kronfeld in Berkeley and mailed me his drafts. I spent many afternoons reading our translations aloud to Yehuda and getting his response. In "A Precise Woman," his feedback was especially helpful. Here the poet writes in praise of his beloved:

> *A precise woman with a short haircut brings order*
> *to my thoughts and my dresser drawers,*
> *moves feelings around like furniture*
> *into a new arrangement.*
> 5   *A woman whose body is cinched at the waist and firmly divided*
> *into upper and lower,*
> *with weather-forecast eyes*
> *of shatterproof glass.*
> *Even her cries of passion follow a certain order,*
> 10   *one after the other:*
> *tame dove, then wild dove,*
> *then peacock, wounded peacock, peacock, peacock,*
> *then wild dove, tame dove, dove dove*
> *thrush, thrush, thrush.*
> 15   *A precise woman: on the bedroom carpet*
> *her shoes always point away from the bed.*
> *(My own shoes point toward it.)*

This is how lines 9-14 sound in Hebrew:

> Afilu tsa'akot ha-ta'avah lefi seder,
> achat acharey ha-shniya ve-lo me'urbavot:
> yonat bayit, achar kakh yonat bar,
> achar kakh tavas, tavas patsua, tavas, tavas.
> Achar kakh yonat bar, yonat bayit, yona yona
> tinshémet, tinshémet, tinshémet.

The word I've translated as "thrush" is *tinshémet* in Hebrew, and its modern dictionary definition is "barn owl," which gives us "barn owl, barn owl, barn owl." What is one to do? I lifted mine eyes unto the Bible, whence help often comes. But *tinshémet* appears only three times in the Bible, and no one seems to know what it means. In Leviticus (11:18) and in Deuteronomy

(14:6), the *tinshémet*, along with the vulture and the bat, is listed among the unclean birds that we are prohibited from eating; in the Bibles I consulted, it is translated variously as "swan" (KJV), "water hen" (Revised Standard Version), and "little owl" (New English Bible). To add to the confusion, in Leviticus 11:30, the *tinshémet* appears in a list of unclean creeping things; here I found it translated as "mole" (KJV) and "chameleon" (RSV, NEB).

When I turned back to the Hebrew, it struck me that Amichai was not thinking of any of these "abominations." I asked him whether he chose *tinshémet* for its sound as well as its meaning, and he confirmed my guess. *Tinshémet* is based on the root *nasham*, "to breathe," and in this context, the sibilant *sh* suggests breathing, or, I should say, heavy breathing. So I found "thrush," perched between albatross and zebra finch, in my trusty thesaurus. But since I'm a little shaky on the names of birds–I know a hawk from a handsaw and an owl from a pussycat, that's about it–I was relieved to see that Webster's identifies the thrush as a European bird, which brings it within Amichai's purview. Then I discovered, in his "Seven Laments for the War Dead," that Amichai once read about the thrush in an old German zoology text. And so it came to pass that the lady recovers from her passion–in English–like a thrush. This example shows that what's called a "free" translation is usually not, as you might suppose, the result of an unfettered flight of the imagination. When you're translating a poem of Amichai's, you open the Bible (or rather, the Bibles), the concordance, the dictionary, the thesaurus, the complete works of the poet–and let your fingers do the walking. Only then can you fly.

Chana Kronfeld and I were honored when Amichai asked us to translate *Open Closed Open* (2000), his magnum opus, and sadly, his last book. I'd like to say a word about our process of collaboration on *Open Closed Open*, and more recently on *Hovering at a Low Altitude: The Collected Poetry of Dahlia Ravikovitch* (2009). Even if my Hebrew weren't rusty –which it is–it would never be as good as that of a native speaker. Chana is a native speaker of Hebrew and I of English, so our debates on language and its context gave a real sense of meaning to current theories about translation as a negotiation between cultures. Our method was dialogue: in the way that Talmudic scholars study a text together by raising alternative possibilities, we debated every word and every turn of phrase. In those intense and absorbing conversations, we often had the feeling that Hebrew and English language and culture were talking to each other over the divide, and that together we were enacting a border crossing.

Some of the time I would prepare rough drafts as a starting point. Then Chana would explain what I missed: "This line comes from the Talmud, and this is a pop song, and this is army slang, and this is children's talk, and this line comes from a skit in the 1980s that everyone knew." Readers outside Israel have tended to oversimplify the meaning of Amichai's work, to blunt his irony, the critical edge of his Hebrew, and even to present him as a religious poet. We were determined to render the full range of his voices, from the colloquial to the densely allusive, while retaining in English the natural ease of his poetic idiom.

Chana would talk about the nuances of words and their cultural context, and I would struggle with what English can and cannot convey. Often she would urge me to push against the boundaries of English, to enlarge, if only slightly, the receptivity of English to Amichai's or Ravikovitch's "otherness" of style, to give the foreignness a tangible presence in the poem, resisting the common tendency to bleach out the cultural particularity. This is a rhetorical strategy that Walter Benjamin famously advocates in his essay, "The Task of the Translator," to "expand and deepen [one's] language by means of the foreign language." Through my work with Chana, I've come to appreciate more deeply the value of this approach, which is gaining recognition in current theories of translation. If you travel to another place, you should come back with something you couldn't find at home. This assumes that the reader is willing to make a bit of an effort, but why assume otherwise?

Amichai's "I Studied Love" is part of a sequence, "Gods Change, Prayers Are Here to Stay," where he boldly takes the measure of the Orthodox Jewish practices he grew up with. Here he writes that he learned about love in the Orthodox synagogue of his childhood, with its strict separation of the sexes and subordination of women, by studying the women "on the other side" of the partition:

> *I studied love in my childhood in my childhood synagogue*
> *in the women's section with the help of the women behind the partition*
> *that locked up my mother with all the other women and girls.*
> *But the partition that locked them up locked me up*
> *on the other side. They were free in their love while I remained*
> *locked up with all the men and boys in my love, my longing.*
> *I wanted to be there with them and to know their secrets*
> *and say with them, "Blessed be He who has made me*
> *according to his will." And the partition–*
> *a lace curtain white and soft as summer dresses, swaying*

> *on its rings and loops of wish and would,*
> *lu-lu loops, lullings of love in the locked room.*
> *And the faces of women like the face of the moon behind the clouds*
> *or the full moon when the curtain parts: an enchanted*
> *cosmic order. At night we said the blessing*
> *over the moon outside, and I*
> *thought about the women.*

Why is the poet so busily studying the women's faces in the synagogue? Isn't the purpose of the partition to keep him from doing just that, to keep him focused on his prayers? The Hebrew for partition is *mechitza*. That rabbinic term comes from the root *chatza*, "to cut, divide, or cross a dividing line." In modern Hebrew *chutz la-aretz* means "abroad," *la-chatsot et ha-gvul* means "to cross the border," and the plural form, *mechitzot* "barriers," may occur in the phrase "linguistic and cultural barriers."

The poet describes himself as longing to cross a cultural barrier–a barrier that stopped the translators short. As Naomi Seidman writes, translation is "a border zone," and "what does not succeed in crossing the border is at least as interesting as what makes it across." To most English readers, "Blessed be He who has made me according to His will"–*Baruch she-asani kirtsono*–is unambiguously pious. If they cannot identify this verse as part of the morning prayers recited by women, they will not recognize just how iconoclastic it is–first, because Amichai wishes to say the woman's blessing instead of the man's, and second, because the man's blessing happens to be *Baruch she-lo asani isha*, "Blessed be He who has not made me a woman." In our notes to the poem we quote the man's blessing, though we know that a footnote cannot begin to express how that bit of knowledge radically alters the way the poem reads. More often than not, a note points to a problem rather than resolving it. It signals to the reader: "The following bit of culture-stuff, which we will now define in a few words, is something that cannot be defined in a few words."

In the Song of Songs and in Amichai's "I Studied Love," women are the bearers of a special wisdom about love. Written more than two millennia apart, these works are nothing short of astonishing when read in the context of traditional Jewish culture, where women have been and still are accorded a subordinate role. In the Song, the brothers who rebuke and threaten the Shulamite about her sexual behavior, and the "watchmen of the walls" who assault her, exemplify the social strictures that mark the woman as "Other." The partition in the Orthodox synagogue serves much the same function.

It is Amichai's openness to the Other that enables him to write the poetry of a whole human being–one of the reasons for his immense appeal. "What's it like to be a woman?" he asks in an early poem. In a poem published after the 1967 war, we find him on Yom Kippur, in the Old City of Jerusalem, standing before the shop of an Arab–a notions shop, much like his father's, which was burned down in Germany–trying to make sense of the parallels between the two men and the tragic history that divides them.

Amichai's curiosity about "what it is like / on the other side" reminds me of the question in the poem by Judith with which I began. I don't want to press the comparison too far; the *mechitza*, after all, is not a given of human existence, just one of the many partitions and checkpoints and walls that we humans erect. In Amichai's poem the *mechitza* separates man and woman, and as I have been suggesting, self from Other. Making a translation, or reading one, is about crossing all these boundaries.

Amichai's "I Studied Love" tells us that some essential knowledge about "the other side" is "locked up" behind the *mechitza*, and yet, with effort and empathy, it can be retrieved. The same is true of the knowledge of other ages, other cultures, locked away behind the barriers of language–knowledge that we need in order to be fully human, and that we gain in the act of imaginative understanding that we call translation.

Design and typography by
Chuck Byrne Design,
using Adrian Frutiger's
Meridien types.

400 paperbound copies on
Mohawk Superfine paper.

Printed by Autumn Press.